# GOD NEVER SAYS,
# "YES, BUT..."

Leonard Foley, O.F.M.

*Nihil Obstat*
> Rev. Hilarion Kistner, O.F.M.
> Rev. John J. Jennings

*Imprimi Potest:*
> Rev. Andrew Fox, O.F.M.
> Provincial

*Imprimatur:*
> + Daniel E. Pilarczyk, V.G.
> Archdiocese of Cincinnati
> November 7, 1978

The *Nihil Obstat* and *Imprimatur* are a declaration that a book or pamphlet is considered to be free from doctrinal or moral error. It is not implied that those who have granted the *Nihil Obstat* and *Imprimatur* agree with the contents, opinions or statements expressed.

Cover and illustrations by Julie Van Leeuwen.

SBN 0-912228-53-9

Some people look calmly at the age-old problems and need no more than simple faith. Others, not without faith, are helped by discussion, even if it be in awkward human words. This book is offered to the latter group. Some of them, by their honest doubts and humble spirit, helped in its writing.

# CONTENTS

v

# 1. Guilt

*God never says,
"I forgive you,
but…"*

**T**he door of the Prodigal Son's home had no lock. It stood open, a standing welcome. A hundred times a day the father looked out towards the spot where the road disappeared at the top of a hill.

It would have been useless to send force to drag the boy back. Can you chain a son to his father's table?

Time must pass. Time—a possible friend, a potential enemy. It might blur the memory of a father's strong embrace or it might finally exhaust the delights of reckless freedom and leave only the memory of a changeless love back home.

The father's hope won out, but not without a moment of danger. For the boy came home with two ideas—one good, one bad. He said, "I will go to my father's house," for he had finally realized his father would welcome him. But he had it in his mind to add, "I no longer deserve to be called your son," which was as false as any idea could be.

So one day when his father looked out the door for the millionth time, he saw his son come slowly over the hill. He burst out the door and ran till he was out of breath. They had a bone-cracking embrace and came to the house laughing and crying at the same time. When they reached the door, the son made his confession, "Father, I have sinned against God and against you"—a confession that was honest, contrite and healthy. Then he loosed his arms and let the residue of his agony burst out: "I no longer deserve to be called your son."

In an eye-for-an-eye world, he was right, and the odds are that a jury of his peers would agree with him: "You've proved you're a no-good. Now spend some time as a hired hand here, on probation. Perhaps in five years you can go back to your father's table."

But the father was not to be put off by such barroom justice. *He ignored the statement,* acted as if it had not been said, as if his son had only returned from a concentration camp.

"Quick!" he said to the servants, "bring out the finest robe and put it on him; put a ring on his finger and shoes on his feet. Take the fatted calf and kill it. Let us eat and celebrate because this son of mine was dead and has come back to life. He was lost and is found" (Luke 15:22-24).

This precious parable of Jesus should do two things for us: first, make the unwavering love of God absolutely convincing; second, correct a distorted notion we share with the Prodigal Son, namely, that we are *not really worthy* of a Father's love.

Deep down, many of us tend to think that God can't actually mean it when he says—so we are told—a divinely ardent "I love you" to all of us, and to each of us individually. What he must be saying, surely, is, "Well, yes, I do love you, of course, but..." We may even think that he is saying, "Being God, I have to forgive you, but I really shouldn't, you know." Or even: "I forgive you; that is, I won't treat you as you really deserve!"

It is very important for all of us to explore these obstacles to a child-like confidence in God's wholehearted forgiveness and unstoppable love. It is useless to fill books with biblical examples of God's love and quote the rhapsodies of saints on the wonders of his mercy if we still think—and it seems many people do—that all this has nothing to do with us, because we simply cannot eradicate a basic feeling of unworthiness and guilt. "It's all very beautiful," we are tempted to say—or we can't help saying—"but I just can't believe that God loves *me* personally, no matter who I am or what I've done."

Why? Because in so many ways we distort the image of God. *We've got to get rid of the foggy lenses!*

When you have your eyes examined, the doctor swings a large binocular contraption into position before your face and asks you to peer through two openings. You see a chart of letters, from magnified E to fine print, on the wall. The doctor slips a lens

3

into a slot on the machine, and your vision is clarified or blurred. Then another lens. Better or worse? The doctor continues until he gets the best combination of lenses for you.

Now suppose that, instead of trying to make things clearer, the doctor kept inserting lenses that would make the chart less and less readable until finally you could not even discern the big E.

This is what happens when we consciously or unconsciously filter the real nature of God's love into almost total darkness, and we start saying, with the Prodigal Son, "You're a lovely Father, I suppose, and you probably mean your forgiveness, but I'm really not worthy to be called your son or daughter."

What's the source of this emotional crippledness?

The Swiss theologian/psychologist Paul Tournier, who is not given to wild statements, has made a very sweeping assertion: "All upbringing is a cultivation of a sense of guilt on an intensive scale." He might have added that not only upbringing, but many everyday relationships are shot through with the infliction of guilt. We lay guilt on each other right and left.

So, if we are to rescue God from his sometime-image as the Great Scorekeeper, Sleuth and Shylock in the Sky, or even from the role of cold-blooded Judge in a human court, we will have to come to terms with two distorting lenses that have been slipped over our eyes. *One is the guilt other people inflict on us; the second is what we do to ourselves.* Each of these has clearly distinguishable layers. Only when we have confidently removed these lenses can we face real guilt and meet the God who says, "Yes, I love you!"

## Stranglehold: What Other People Think

As Tournier says, we all grow up in an atmosphere of imposed guilt. Some of this process may be justified. A child must learn, to put the matter in rock bottom terms, that "good must be done and evil avoided," and that stolen candy must be returned.

So, when Mother cuddles little sister and kisses the place where Rodney left his teeth marks and says something no more devastating to him than, "You hurt your sister," he begins to have the elementary feelings of guilt. So far, the feeling is healthy. It may still be healthy if he is penalized two or three play periods as a second offender who still doesn't believe in his sister's right to life, liberty and the pursuit of happiness.

Again, so far so good. But if Mother now proceeds to control him with constant reminders of his guilt ("Be nice to your cousin now—don't do what you did to Sissy!"), he begins to get the idea (1) that his guilt is irremovable and (2) that his own personal worth is going down like water in a sink.

My favorite in this category of inflicted guilt is, "Let's clean the garage for Jesus!" Mother and Dad can't sell the idea on its own merits or their authority so, by a massive overkill, they bring in the most guilt-inducing motive. The child is left with the dismal choice of letting Jesus down or missing the neighborhood ball game.

Parents have been known to simply *declare* a child guilty and in need of confession: "You wasted your food, and that *is* a sin! You should go to confession and tell God what you did."

The parent did not just say it is an evil thing to

waste food, etc., but that the child has consciously and willingly embraced this evil with a moral act. This is simply an impossible judgment for anyone to make about anybody. A parent does not know the deepest awareness or "conscience-ness" of anyone, even his or her own child. Only God knows that. (As a wholesome penance any offending parent should read Haim Ginott's *Between Parent and Child*.).

Another ploy is, "Aren't you ashamed of yourself?" (I wasn't, because I didn't know I was doing anything wrong. Now I am, but for no good reason, only because I was labeled a little criminal.)

And so the child begins a journey that will progressively burden his or her shoulders with other-inflicted guilt. Whatever one may think of Sigmund Freud and his theories, he at least makes us pause when he asserts that all guilt comes from society's pressures.

An experiment in a Canadian school tells an interesting truth: Students did not cheat when they were told they would be on their honor during a test with no teacher present, and the penalty for mistakes would be to write incorrect answers so many times. But the next day the teacher said, "Today there will be no penalties. But I will be very disappointed in anyone who makes mistakes. Students as smart as you should have no trouble." That day there was a lot of head-turning, whispering and plain cheating. At all costs, the children felt obliged to avoid the guilt of letting the teacher down.

We grow up surrounded by the "shoulds" of society. Many of these are wholesome and even essential, of course. One should pay just debts, respect others' rights, contribute a fair share, etc. But other "shoulds" are open to an interpretation based on false values: one must "get someplace" in the world (i.e., make money); a woman should be "fulfilled" (i.e., not have more than two children).

If a man is a good American, he works hard; if he relaxes, he feels guilty. Then he reads that it's mentally healthy to relax, and he feels guilty working.

Many women are embarrassed if someone drops in and sees two unwashed dishes in the sink or a toy on the floor. They feel guilty if their home is not a kind of holy of holies where nary a fleck of cigarette ash ever gets as far as the floor. There are probably even some women who have an uneasy feeling for not doing the wash on *Monday* morning.

Those who are sick feel guilty because they are presumably "putting others out."

Parents feel guilty because their son or daughter isn't on the first team, or a cheerleader, or on the dean's list, or, worst of all, grows up and doesn't make much money, or chooses a "lower" job.

Children can be made to feel terribly guilty for not accomplishing impossible ideals and monumental "shoulds"—straight A's, endless popularity, effortless maturity and an unblemished complexion.

In the office, slow but efficient workers may feel guilty in comparison with speedsters, and the latter feel guilty for being superficial. No one is allowed to have an individual rhythm.

Even religion, or especially religion, occasions guilt. When someone piously tells me that I would have more peace if I prayed better, I simply feel guilty, because I am not exactly at peace. Obviously I am not a good pray-er. Or, "God cures those who put their trust in him," or even, "Are you born again?" may slide me three more notches down on the scale of self-esteem.

The point of all this is not that someone may or may not be actually guilty of wrongdoing, but that the standard is made to be *what other people think*. This is the guilt of a child. It may be the only way a child can be taught the rudiments of responsibility, but the resulting attitude ought to have been long discarded by the mature adult. The latter says: I am not guilty because of what other people think. I may be guilty, but not because they think so. They may or may not be judging by God's standards.

It should be no surprise that the human Jesus had to disassociate himself from this kind of guilt. Even Mary used the time-worn plea of parents, "Why did you do this to us?" Jesus had to declare his need to follow his Father's way even if it conflicted with what well-meaning people *thought:* "Did you not know [read: you should have known] that I must be about my Father's business?"

Jesus was disassociating himself from *false* guilt.

### "I Was Taught That..."

Since much false guilt is induced by "education," some of it can be eradicated by reeducation. That's what happens to most of us. Some people, however, are damaged to their roots, and spend a lifetime of misery. They don't have to "put themselves down"; they're already convinced they're as "down" as they can go.

Parents who do not (or cannot) show children the full picture of God's laws and the gospel understanding of morality may leave them with a set of erroneous moral principles that can lead to untold anguish and discouragement: "I missed Mass [i.e., I was in bed with 105 degree fever], therefore I am guilty of mortal sin." Or, "I had sexual thoughts [i.e., I am human], therefore I am guilty of having bad thoughts and desires." Or, "I don't go to daily Mass [i.e., I have eight children], therefore I must not be a very good Catholic." Or, "My baby is sick— this must be punishment for my sins." "I see Pete Nitney isn't going to church any more [because of a terrible emotional problem I don't know about]; he's living in mortal sin."

These examples may seem exaggerated in the present climate of the Church, but anyone who deals with others' conscience problems will recognize a mentality that still affects many Catholics—an external, almost magical view of religion, and a wary notion of God that sees him as a steel-hearted employer who pays minimum wages to those who work overtime and who has spies all over the shop to report slackers.

This God doesn't say, "Yes, I love you." He says, "Back to the salt mines, and no nonsense!"

Low self-esteem may be the most widespread affliction suffered by the human race, but God didn't plan it that way. Babies are supposed to learn they are important persons if mother and father hold them, kiss them, hover and gurgle over them like guardian angels. This is the only way any of us ever got the notion we were worthwhile. Because we got such assurance, we could easily believe in a God who is even more enthusiastic about us than our parents are.

But if a baby, a child, never or seldom gets this

affirmation, there is a tragic result: "I am no good. I see others being loved, but I am not. I must be worthless. Because I have nothing to give, I cannot love others. When they tell me they love me, I know they are just saying words, because I am not worth loving." How can such a person believe in a loving God?

## The Opposite Extreme: "Who, Me?"

At the opposite extreme from letting others inflict guilt on me is the refusal to admit the sinfulness of which I am really guilty. The most tragic sin is to put a distorting lens between ourselves and our real sin.

Jesus' greatest anger was reserved for those who were presumably the most "religious," the self-made saints who claimed no sin: "Woe to you scribes and Pharisees, you frauds! You are like white-washed tombs, beautiful to look at on the outside but inside full of filth and dead men's bones" (Matthew 23:25, 27).

He was echoing Jeremiah, "Behold, I will judge you on that word of yours, 'I have not sinned'" (2:35b), and would be himself echoed by John:

If we say, "We are free of the guilt of sin,"
we deceive ourselves; the truth is not to be found
in us....
If we say, "We have never sinned,"
we make him a liar
and his word finds no place in us."

(I John 1:8, 10).

It almost seems that we are able to sin only by denying our sin. I doubt that anybody in all history

10

ever sat himself down and said, "Now, I want to be very clear about this: it is a serious matter, and I undoubtedly have, and want to have, full knowledge and full consent of my will." Rather we must maneuver ourselves into self-deception. We must be Adam and Eve, not really "disobeying" God, just seeking a knowledge of good and evil.

We know we are guilty, but we refuse to know it. We are like the young Augustine and his outrageous prayer (if he really said it): "Lord, give me chastity, but not yet."

But murder will out, one way or another. Denying my real guilt doesn't give me any satisfaction. I can't really enjoy my sin, even if "it isn't any sin." The denial or repression of guilt only makes things worse. It is a festering beneath the surface and an emptiness in the heart. Blinded and afraid, I rebel in irritation, stubbornness, aggressiveness.

Obviously such an attitude can have no real relationship with a forgiving Father. When he was leaving home, the Prodigal Son could not look his father in the eye as he received his money, and he couldn't think about home when he was having his own way in the big city.

Sin is choosing to deny reality and living in a world of our own creation. Whether we are nurturing resentment, indulging selfishness or clinging to counterfeit passions, we must block a just and merciful God out of our consciousness. Our minds and hearts were made for truth and love. These natural impulses, graced in Christ, must be denied if we are to maintain our sinning.

We *choose* not to believe, in such an atmosphere of suspended reality, that God is a kindly Father waiting at the door. We cannot afford to think of that, because it would spoil whatever satisfaction we think we are enjoying. We must make God into a convenient image: unreasonable, uninterested or simply not present.

The other side of the coin of denied guilt is the pharisaical attitude which may in fact be guiltless of all but the most fundamental sin: self-sufficiency before God. This is the spirit that is concerned only with being very sure that God doesn't have anything "on" me. I am constantly proving my right to have a relationship with God. I deserve it, because I am so virtuous, perfectly observant of the law, so strong and superior. In this case God has an *obligation* to say Yes to me.

It's not grace or mercy, but a debt. It's not a kindly, forgiving, grieving Father who patiently waits for my return, but a business partner giving me my "share." I get my money at the window, and then go about displaying the virtue I have created.

Jesus had words for those who would not admit their sickness, sin or human limitation: "I have come to heal those who are sick, not the righteous." It's too bad they didn't realize he was calling them *self*-righteous.

### The Sickness of "It's Only Venial Sin"

Finally, there are those semi-tragic persons who are neither full-fledged Pharisees nor total sinners abandoned to self-will and blindness; neither lost in a dark prison of false guilt nor totally open and free in God's mercy as fully admitted sinners.

These are the people many of us see when we

look—not too searchingly—into the mirror. We may be basically turned to God as, say, a husband and wife who are deeply in love with each other. But there is still a part of ourselves that is not totally given to him. We call this our "minor" selfishness, petty vindictiveness, lack of discipline, laziness, etc. Husbands and wives may be ready to die for each other, but they are also capable of occasionally nasty quarrels. These stormy sessions (or long silences) do not destroy their basic love—ultimately they can, of course—but represent an infection in a generally healthy relationship.

So also, I can in large part face God honestly. But I have the peculiar ability to avoid his eye a little bit. This is the Catholic heresy that says something is "only a venial sin." True, it is no more comparable to the guilt of mortal sin than one cancer cell is to dying of the illness. Yet it is a fact. It shares, no matter how lightly, in the denied guilt of the great sinner.

Such people—we—smile at the threats of ardent preachers. Venial sin does *not* add up to mortal sin: it says so right in the catechism. There really is no parallel, we tell ourselves, between the attitude of mortal and of venial sin. It can't happen to me. And God, like a harried orphanage director, will never miss the small percentage of love I withhold from him.

What else can account for our restless lives? We too have distorting lenses, perhaps the hardest of all to be rid of: "My laziness is not a real failing; it's my temperament." Or, "My vindictiveness is really a kind of courage that marks me off from those who let people get away with things." Or, "My selfishness is simply the recognition that I actually do deserve a bit more than the ordinary mortal."

And so it is not God who says, "Yes, but..." It is our timid, grasping selves.

## Why Real, Admitted Guilt is Healthy

It is paradoxical that for almost everyone the healthiest emotional-mental attitude is that of real guilt. It is a plain admission of factual bad will, free choice of evil, denial of truth. It is not concerned with what other people think. It no longer avoids God's eyes, it makes no pretense of having put God in debt by any good works. It simply lets down all defenses (what a great relief!) and stands under the judgment of God.

The secular mind finds it impossible to believe that when this happens there is no longer any fear of God's judgment or punishment. The mind is made for truth and the heart for love, and when we turn from untruth and the refusal to love we are back in the atmosphere for which we were made, like fish in water. The fire and brimstone are gone. We are not "sinners in the hands of an angry God." We know very well that we no longer "deserve to be called your son or daughter," but we know even better that this is beside the point. God doesn't think in those terms. He doesn't love us because we have deserved his love, but because he *is* Love.

We become humble enough to accept forgiveness without having "deserved" it by our own self-propelled regimen of penance and purification. We are simply children, weak and wounded, with no way of healing ourselves—but now we are safe and secure in

14

our Father's loving arms.

St. John continued the statement quoted above with:

> But if we acknowledge our sins,
> he who is just can be trusted
> to forgive our sins
> and cleanse us from every wrong. (I John 1:9)

If we admit our guilt in a fully human way—no reservations, no excuses, no minimizing or exaggerating—it becomes the real guilt that disappears in God's mercy. It is only because I *do not* sincerely ask God to be forgiven that there is, on my part, the slightest chill in the relationship. The problem is not that I am afraid of my weakness, that I might repeat the sin; it is not that I am afraid of God—I know very well who God is. The simple fact is that all unhappiness in life results from my refusing some part of my life—substantial or "small"—to the loving embrace of God.

The remedy is to accept from Jesus the grace of truth—and to be free.

## "I Have Come That You May Have the Truth"

The center of time, the spot where all eyes, distortion-free, can focus, is Jesus, God's visible, audible, touchable "Yes!" to his children.

Jesus comforted the afflicted, including those bowed down with false guilt, and afflicted the comfortable, those who would not admit their sin and who claimed virtue was the work of their own hands.

He looked about him and saw crippled men and women: some with shriveled hearts, picking at their sin and assuring themselves that they were happy;

15

others huddled in a dark cave of fear where others had imprisoned them.

It was the latter he saw when he looked on the crowd and "pitied them, for they were like sheep without a shepherd" (Mark 6:34a). They were lost, confused, unsure of themselves, doubtful of God's mercy. Hearing only words of blame from the pious, they could not help feeling they were guilty of their loneliness and fear.

Jesus told them the Good News that God loves them. Not "even" them, but "especially" them. He came that they might have the truth of God's compassionate love, and be freed from "what others think."

But to the willfully blind Jesus had to change his manner. Even so, his sternness to the pious hypocrites of his day was an act of love. He was like a doctor cutting into the windpipe of someone choking to death.

"Woe to you scribes and Pharisees, you frauds! You cleanse the outside of cup and dish, and leave the inside filled with loot and lust! You are like whitewashed tombs, beautiful to look at on the outside, but inside full of filth and dead men's bones" (Matthew 23:25, 27).

This was not God saying "Yes, but..." It was a God insisting on truth: Admit that you are not really in tune with truth and love. Admit that you, not the people you preach to, need healing, forgiveness. Admit the emptiness in your heart. Let go self-sufficiency. Accept the relief of admitting what you are!

The placidly venial sinners, always in danger of becoming Pharisees, also met with Jesus' healing wrath. "How I wish you were one or the other—hot or cold!" he said (Revelation 3:15b). There is at least something decisive about a "big" sinner. "But because you are lukewarm... I will spew you out of my mouth!" (Revelation 3:16).

Again, this is not God saying "Yes, but..." He is saying: You have an infection in your love that has not yet strangled its life. But it can. Do not play with my love. I want your whole self, for *your* sake. I don't want to forgive you *somewhat*. I want to heal you of everything—all your reluctance, childishness, immaturity, flirting with evil. I want you totally, not almost, at peace.

Paradoxically, only those who had the humility to open themselves to forgiveness really appreciated how guilty they had been. They felt themselves released from something far worse than they had been willing to admit. Only when they realized that God loved them *absolutely* did they also realize the tragedy of cutting themselves off from him. For the worst punishment sin brings with itself is the denial of sin and the burial of guilt.

And so the sinners were the freest with Jesus. He ate and drank with them—the crooked lawyers and moneylenders, the harlots and adulterers, the cruel and the greedy. They laughed and sang and were free. And the pious looked on in dismay.

But even the freed had to be careful. It was still possible for them to fall into the opposite error: that God now loved only *them,* only the really guilty who had finally become really contrite—and no longer loved all those evil people out there so obstinate in their guilt.

For once God does say, "Yes, but..."

"Yes, but I do still love them."

# 2. God's Will, Conscience

*God never says,
"You are free,
but…"*

**G**od did something none of us would do. He put four billion people on this lovely planet and said to each of them, "Choose life. Make up your mind. Take your life into your hands and decide to accept my gift of friendship. I give you freedom: Use it!"

We would have been more orderly. We would not have taken the chance of someone's spoiling the show. We would have *made sure* everyone did what we wanted, because that would be good for them, wouldn't it? Why give people freedom if they may hurt themselves or others? Play it safe. No free will, just a well-programmed universe of beautiful beings whose vocabulary contains only the right words, whose acts automatically follow an eternal plan—and whose lives are about as interesting as a billion books with blank pages.

God couldn't love a machine, or feel honored by a clockwork universe. We can't either, and that's why we really should have no trouble with God's making people free. We have all felt the deep satisfaction of being loved—of having someone who doesn't expect to be paid, or repaid; who is not trying to impress us; who has not been bribed, pressured, cajoled or commanded to love us; who does not "get anything out of it" except the pleasure of unselfish loving. They just love us, period.

Could God be satisfied with anything less? One might say the whole point of Jesus' saving us was to liberate us from being slaves, either cringing or sullen, and to make us his friends.

But friends are equals. It's not a creator-creature relationship. True, and mysterious. The flow of goodness between us and God is really a one-way affair. All that we give back to God is what he gave us in the first place, but now humanized by his grace.

Yet God made us as "equal" to him as he could. He gave us a share in his life. He took our flesh, inseparably, forever. And he gives us the respect of friendship: He will not force himself upon us.

He gives us more than enough reason to trust him—that is, to use our freedom to give ourselves totally to him, and thus be really free. To throw our lives into his hands is not a rash or naive act. But it must be a free act.

A free, trusting act (which joins many other such

20

acts to make up our life) demands a "space" between us and God, a little darkness and separation, if you will. Otherwise, were we to see God face to face immediately, our freedom would be overwhelmed by his beauty and goodness and loveableness.

This "darkness" or "space" is not the self-inflicted darkness of a sinful attitude: We've brought *that* on ourselves. Rather, it is God's standing respectfully outside our door, as it were, politely waiting for us to answer his ring. We know very well who's there, and all he has done for us. We know very much about him, for we have seen his face in hundreds of loving people.

But we don't quite know all about him—so there is an element of trust in opening the door.

## Opening Doors to God's Will

Now, if the comparison is not too farfetched, let's use the "open-the-door-please" policy of God as an entrance to the problem of "God's will."

Until we get to heaven, we won't really open any door and meet God face to face. But we do have to keep opening all sorts of doors to learn more about this Friend-before-all-friends. If we love him, trust him in this space of darkness called mortal life, then we want to learn how to please him. Lovers have been doing that since Adam and Eve.

Now even with those we know and love the best, we do have a problem deciding *which* gift to give them for Christmas or their birthday. It takes some thinking over, and ultimately a decision.

So it is with God. We don't automatically know what is the *precise* loving thing to do *here and now.*

We have to (more or less) *dig* for information, do some *deliberating* (among alternatives), *decide* what to do, and then *do* it.

Later in this chapter we will discuss these "Four D's," which may be helpful in describing the process of maintaining a loving personal relationship with God: dig, deliberate, decide and do.

These elements are involved in "forming" our conscience. Implied is this: What pleases God is not always evident immediately. "God's will" is not always black and white, one-and-one-is-two.

That's where the problem arises. Many people think conscience is like an automatic relay system, a kind of computerized response. You punch the buttons and the answer appears on the read-out screen: Money + not mine = don't take. Drowning person + life preserver = throw it! Red traffic light + my car = stop.

But what if it's your friend's money? Can you presume he won't mind? What if it's been stolen from the company? Must you "take it" in order to return it?

What if there are several persons drowning? Who gets the life preserver?

What if a doctor or a priest is on the way to a critically ill person and sees no cars coming from either direction?

What is "God's will" in these cases? What is the free, loving, responsible thing to do? How does God want me to make up my mind, use my freedom?

### Freedom Depends on Knowledge

The trouble is, we really don't like to think. We

prefer to look up the answer in the back of the book.

*The* answer—that's the trouble. We want *the* answer, as if there is only one, always. It's sticky to realize that there may be *an* answer, and *an*other answer. It probably started in our school days, with those mathematics books that had *the* answer in the back. Or with those multiple-choice tests (When was Lincoln born: 1799? 1809? 1819?) in which we had to get *the* answer.

When it came to catechism, the immaturity of children called for black-and-white moral principles: Yes, you may do this; no, you may not do that. This is a sin, that is not—and that was *the* answer.

But then came those Philadelphia-lawyer religion classes in high school. How much meat do you have to eat on Friday to commit a mortal sin? How long can you kiss a girl? If you steal $17 from Rockefeller, is it a mortal sin?

Adulthood brought the realization that there is an answer to many questions, and that there are some moral situations in which *the* answer is obvious and absolute; but the application of general principles ("Love your neighbor") is often perplexing. How long do you wait before turning a drug addict over to public authority? Should you maintain a close friendship with someone who is cheating his employees? Should you continue going to neighborhood parties in spite of the somewhat coarse moral atmosphere?

When a moral aspect is not obvious, people make the most complex decisions with relatively strong confidence: They open a new business, take a different job, move to another city, buy a car, or bet the daily double.

But in situations which clearly have a moral content, many people are either overly worried or falsely complacent about a magic thing called "God's will." They think it's something *already settled,* like a photo already taken: It's in the negative, and needs only to be developed.

Should I take the job with Neutron Bombs, Inc.? Well, the magic attitude says, it's all in the heavenly zillion-page book of "God's will." The trick is to find the right page and number. You squeeze your eyes shut, hold your breath, grit your teeth, and the answer pops into your head: No, it's not God's will that I go with Neutron Bombs. What God has decided from all eternity is that I now work for Knitting Kneedles Ltd.

Of course a pat answer, magically arrived at, saves a lot of anxious probing and the agony of decisions. Should I put my mother in a nursing home? Get Father Whoozis to decide it for me. What about loaning my brother-in-law $500? Light a candle. Should I tell off the nasty clerk or go away quietly? Flip a coin.

We like to settle things, not by getting advice (which everyone, including the Pope, must do) and thinking, but by getting the answer from some outside source—a priest, a psychiatrist or Ann Landers.

But if we are to take God's gifts seriously, it seems evident that his "will" is that we use what he has given us: amazing intelligence and free choice. It is true that we start with some "givens": love your neighbor, be patient, pray, help the poor, bear fruit in charity, etc. But the specifics of these general commandments must be the result of our well-made judgments, not a magic answer pulled from a hat.

## What About "Special" Signs From God?

The first question to be dealt with in this regard is that of "special" signs from God that some people feel they receive. Now, no minor scribbler like myself is going to tell God that he can't give people special signs if he wants, just as he can answer prayers any way he wants. If God wants to send an angel to pick up the prophet Habakkuk by the hair and put him down in the lions' den many miles away, no one dare say this is not according to the "normal ways of Providence." If St. Francis opens the Bible three times and finds the same call to poverty, I'm not going to argue that this was a mere coincidence. And if Paul of Tarsus is blinded by a light brighter than the sun on his way to Damascus, I'm not going to argue that he imagined it.

But, at the risk of sounding like a rationalist, I think there is danger in looking for "special" signs from God. He has given us Jesus, and Jesus has remained visible in his loving community, and that should be enough revelation for anybody.

The Church has always insisted that we do not have to believe in any private revelation, even that of Lourdes. And if anyone wants to find out how "rationalistic" the Church can be, let him try to claim that a "miracle" was worked at that lovely shrine. The Church insists that every natural explanation must be exhausted before there can be any question of a "special" intervention of God.

Speaking of the discernment of extraordinary mystical phenomena, the Dominican theologian Father Jordan Aumann writes in the *New Catholic Encyclopedia:* "No extraordinary phenomenon may be attributed to a supernatural, i.e., divine, cause as long as a natural or diabolical explanation is possible . . . . Normally it would be temerarious to petition God for charisms or miracles, since none of these phenomena flow from sanctifying grace, the virtues, and the gifts of the Holy Ghost; and privileges of this kind could in fact be damaging to the spiritual life of an individual."

It is not necessarily heretical, then, to be a little wary about declaring that some given event or experience is undoubtedly a special sign of God's will. That your son bumps into a Dominican two hours after you've discussed religious vocations at the dinner table is not necessarily a sign that God wants him to join that illustrious order. If you can't find your cigarettes on Ash Wednesday, that is not necessarily a sign God wants you to give up smoking.

Come to think of it, there is even a wee bit of danger of some wishful thinking here. I happen to open a book at the chapter on "Fraternal Correction" and may therefore be sure that God wants me to tell off Joe McGillicuddy once and for all. When the sun breaks through the clouds and starts to warm up the golf course, that is not necessarily God telling me to stop trying to write this difficult book and go out and hit a few.

What then?

Jesus told us to read the signs of the times. Note that the word "signs" is plural, and so is "times." There are many signs of God's will. In fact, I think we can profitably avoid the pitfalls of seeing "special" signs by reading the "ordinary, all-the-time" signs.

When people say that the Holy Spirit suddenly

told them to go visit Room 205 in Bethesda Hospital (no matter who's in there), I have a diabolical temptation to ask, "And what was the Holy Spirit telling you the minute before this 'suddenly' happened?" Or the hour before? Or the day before? What is the Holy Spirit doing in between these sudden inbursts into our consciousness? Resting? Busy elsewhere?

We are back to the biblical mentality: *God is busy all the time. Everything is a sign from God,* if I choose to read it in the light of the gospel. There are hundreds of other "signs" to interpret besides bumping into the Dominican.

I don't have to lose my Camels on Ash Wednesday to know that I'm smoking too much and that God is telling me all the time to take care of my body.

The fact is, I have more evidence of what God wants than I sometimes care to examine. And the itch to learn special secrets from God somehow contradicts the very nature of faith: trusting the God who has abundantly revealed himself in Jesus.

### Back to the Drawing Board

It would seem, then, that there may be some hard work involved in discerning God's will.

If God has given me freedom, he must want me to use it. Freedom is inextricably joined to my intelligence, my emotions and my body. God wants me to *decide*, personally and with my whole person.

Just as God has what might be called a "general" loving will, so he wants me to respond to his offer of friendship with a *fundamental* or basic choice to love in return. Theologians today call this our "fundamental option." It is the decision-that-results-from-many-decisions. It is what I become, by all the little choices I make in my life. My fundamental option or decision puts God's love first and all else second. It is the most powerful ingredient of all my decisions.

As I grow into this fundamental attitude, I am a child of God, I am "born again," I am in the "state" of grace. (Obviously, there can be a gradually formed fundamental option in the *other* direction, which is the gradually formed decision of mortal sinfulness. My basic relationship with God slowly dies, because my coalescing decisions become the fundamental decision to go my own way. Such a decision can express itself in a deliberate campaign of lies to discredit my business competitors.)

If one has accepted this basic love which God constantly tries to create in us, all other decisions follow easily, as far as sincerity and generosity are concerned. Because I simply love God, I can "mean well" in all other decisions.

But it's not enough to mean well. No one ever goes to a "sincere" surgeon who doesn't know a scalpel from a putty knife. And if the new immigrant from Malagasy drives on the left side of the road, we don't let him continue because he "means well."

There is a virtue designed to take care of both meaning well and doing the right thing. It's called the virtue of prudence.

There it is, that poor-relation word that we've tended to put in the back room. "Prudence" has had a bad, even a slanderous press. Prudence, many think, is being "chicken." It means going back six times to see if the door is really locked.

It means being the last one to take off your long underwear in May, and the first one to put on the storm windows in late August. "Prudent" mothers don't let their kids play outside beyond their watchful eyes. "Prudent" lovers won't go on a date until they have a complete print-out from Pre-Marital Profiles, Inc. "Prudent" people never sail uncharted seas or drill new oil wells.

But real prudence is a very solid intellectual virtue, and it has everything to do with God's will. Prudence is the virtue whereby we do our best to make right decisions of conscience. It simply says, "If you're going to buy the Brooklyn Bridge, ask some knowledgeable people about the going price of bridges, take an expert along to examine the rivets, find out the history of other bridges, when they collapse, how often they need paint." It would be highly *im*prudent to buy the Brooklyn Bridge without taking the time to find out all the *facts* on which a reasonable decision can be made.

A prudent conscience decision, of course, begins with an attitude of faith and a sincere desire to please God. It desires to act responsibly, to do the loving thing called for at this moment. According to the weightiness of the decision (you don't take two hours deciding whether God wants you to have chocolate or vanilla ice cream), you take time to find out the facts of the situation.

### The Four D's

More to the point: A conscience decision—we make hundreds of them every day—is prudent when it has had the four D's referred to above: dig, deliberate, decide and do. (We are presuming the "general" good will, an attitude of faith, a sincere desire to please God, the overall "responsible response" to God's call.)

## 1) Dig

If even the Pope doesn't know something—say, what the *Godspell* cast is planning to do during an audience at St. Peter's—he must ask some knowledgeable person, perhaps his teenage nephew, before walking out on the stage and possibly making a fool of himself.

If a principal is going to investigate a classroom ruckus, his first obligation is to find out what actually happened, who was there, what exactly was said, what special circumstances pertained.

Before we make a decision, prudence demands that we use the old familiar list: who, what, where, when, why, how. Mature people almost unconsciously answer all these questions with more than computer speed. Here are examples (among 36 possible) of one of the questions for each of six situations:

I'm going to say something. *Who* is here that I may unjustly offend?

*What* is involved in taking the baby-sitting job?

*Where* are we? I can't bring up things at a friend's house that belong to our own family circle.

*Why* was the fence put up? I should know the reason before I take it down.

*When* should I mention that someone left the Frigidaire door open all night?

And so on and on, a thousand times a day. What

should I wear when we go visit this poor family? If I work until midnight, should I feel guilty if I don't make an hour's meditation? If someone has just gotten up and is bleary-eyed at the breakfast table, should I try to discuss nuclear proliferation, Genesis II or possible divorce? (I have a friend who, as we enter Riverfront Stadium to watch the Bengals trounce the Steelers, always comes up with something like "Do you really think St. Mark's Gospel was written before St. Matthew's?)

Obviously, if all I'm trying to decide is whether to stroll on the right or left side of Fillmore Park, I don't spend days with landscape charts, meteorological tables or grass-cutting records. But if I'm to drive off to Florida after the wedding, intending to start a window-washing business (You think I'm making this up?) to support myself and spouse, then I'd better have asked some serious "who-what-when-where-why-how's."

## 2) Deliberate

I know the facts, or as many as necessary. I am aware of the situation. Now I have several alternatives: I can make a direct, blunt approach; I can lead up to the subject delicately; I can do it myself or send somebody; I can express my feelings or ask for his or hers; I can wait until tomorrow or until next year.

Which is the *loving* thing to do? Which alternative is the *good* thing to do under the circumstances? What does the good of the Kingdom, the benefit of my friends and enemies and myself, call for? Prudence may call for standing up like St. Peter and saying, "We can't obey your law. Put us in jail if you will." Prudence can lead to crucifixion. If the early (or late) Christians had been more "diplomatic" (phony prudence, timidity), there never would have been any martyrs.

Imprudence would involve not taking enough time to know all the alternatives, or giving them only superficial attention.

### 3) Decide

The purpose of free will is to decide what to do with our life, by the million little decisions that compose it. I know the facts, I know (with whatever shrewdness, wisdom, intelligence and imagination I have) which alternative seems to me to be the loving thing to do *now.*

*Forming* my conscience means bringing it down to this particular form (decision) at this moment. Already present is all my general knowledge of what God has said and done, what I have learned in family and Church, all the experiences of my life, the facts of the moment and the possible alternatives. Now it is time to *choose* one alternative (which may be to do nothing).

### 4) Do

This advice prescription is very simple. If I decide it ought to be done, I ought to do it. Not just talk about it, *do* it.

### So . . . God's Will

I now propose to you, that what I have just tried to describe is the method of knowing and doing what is "God's will." God gave me a mind and free will, and the presumption is that he expects me to use them. I don't think he intended that I hang around Fifth and Vine until a note comes floating down from the sky saying, "Go to Nieman-Marcus and watch for a man wearing a purple coat and a yellow hat. He'll tell you what seminary to enter." I don't think he meant me to flip a coin to decide whether I should marry Appolonia or Hermione. It's hardly probable that I should take every fifth word of the Bible to decide whether to paint my house black or blue.

My mind is made for seeking truth, asking questions, finding facts, estimating probabilities, trying to drink richly from the kaleidoscopic world around me; then to select from all this information whatever I need to love my neighbor (and therefore God) here and now. He gave me a free will to use, that is to decide, to take this course rather than that one (always at a risk). If he meant my will to react as automatically as an electric eye, then he couldn't say, "Well done, good and faithful servant" or "Get lost, you cursed one, for I was hungry and you decided not to share your food."

What the problem comes down to, I submit, is simply this: *God's will is my prudent decision,* or, *God's will is that I make a prudent decision.* St. Paul told the Romans: ". . . be transformed by the renewal of your mind, so that you may judge what is God's will, what is good, pleasing and perfect" (Romans 12:2).

If my decision is as prudent as I can make it, that's what God wants. I am acting humanly—that is, open to the light of truth (which includes facts) and taking my response-ability seriously.

Jesus had no patience with the fearful man who buried his talent in the ground. I cannot bury my ability to decide in a timid, or lazy, reliance on the way the wind is blowing at the present moment. My sister can't make my act of faith, my dad can't admit my guilt, and my mother can't graft her kindness onto my heart.

*God's will is that I prudently decide.* If I do, I'm holy. It may happen that the decision doesn't prove to be economically profitable. The stock I bought, after long research, hits bottom. The car I bought, after much shopping, turns out to be a lemon. I asked myself whether I should look for my son, and decided that he was surely in the other car, riding back with Uncle Tom. Then I had to spend a couple of agonized days looking for him back in Kansas City, and found him at Hebrew College astounding a professor with questions about the book of Isaiah.

In all these cases my decision was prudent, and that's all God asks of anybody.

### What Would Jesus Do?

We can invite unnecessary difficulties if we try to decide what Jesus would do in our shoes. Would Jesus go to Nora Kleinschmidt's cocktail party? Would he read *Time* magazine or watch Carol Burnett? Would he complain about the neighbor's dog or buy a crock pot? Would he drink a Manhattan or play pool? Would he ever decide to take a nap instead of going to the rabbi's lecture?

Jesus is not asking me to do what he would do. He *lived* in a totally different culture. What he is asking of me is to *decide* what to do *with his kind of love* of the Father, his consuming zeal for the Kingdom, his endless compassion for the suffering, his delight in all his Father's creation, his courage in facing opposition and suffering. In short, he asks me to live by his spirit, and by his Spirit.

His Spirit doesn't give me answers, only the intelligence and the light to find the best answer I can under the circumstances. This of course means prayer and a spirit of prayer. The Spirit doesn't take over my free will, but only offers to empower it, make it truly free—*if* I am willing to accept this gift.

My mind is not a note pad on which God writes messages. I am not a ventriloquist's dummy. God asks me to be totally open to his truth and love, and totally enslaved, possessed by his Spirit, accepting his grace as *humanly* as possible. To decide freely is to be human. To decide freely with the light and love of the Spirit is the greatest human thing I can do.

Humble, persistent prayer is the atmosphere in which "God's will" becomes more evident. We can judge and decide most freely in the Spirit when we let God free us of self-sufficiency, prejudice, resentment, dissipation, hurry, self-indulgence, and when we realize we are totally dependent on him.

Then, too, we can much more easily face the comparatively less serious problem of deciding which of two or more possible choices should be made.

> Anyone who loves me
> will be true to my word,
> and my Father will love him;
> we will come to him
> and make our dwelling place with him.

(John 14:23)

36

*Anyone who loves me.* To love is to give and receive humanly, that is, intelligently and freely, using the greatest gifts God gave us.

What God is saying, then, is: "I gave you a head. Use it. I gave you the ability to choose. Choose. Do it with my light and my power. If you do that, I back you up."

God's will, amazing but often undramatic, is *my* prudent decision.

# 3. Suffering

*God never says,*
*"I love you,*
*but…"*

**T**he young widow must put on a brave front. Her three little tots must have a comforting explanation of the strange new atmosphere in the home.

"God wanted Daddy to be with him, so he took him up to heaven, and he's very happy there. We'll all see him again some day."

She is saying, with great faith, "God is good, even though he 'took' my husband. God is with me in this tragedy. It doesn't ruin my life—there is still meaning in it. My husband is still living. I can go on with my life, loving him and others. We will be reunited.

I don't understand how, but somehow, in God's wisdom and love, things will work out."

She has caught the spirit of the totally trusting Jesus in Gethsemane and on the cross: "Father, not my will but yours. I put my life into your hands—whatever happens."

This discussion could end right now, and perhaps it should, by saying that the only real answer to suffering in the world is the cross of Jesus. It's not an explanation, but an action: God takes our problem upon himself.

In a colony of people with leprosy, the leader's encouragement will have much more impact if he suffers the disease himself. Wounded soldiers will take their general's comforting more easily if he is flat on his back just as they are.

So God entered all our human woes except sin. Jesus let himself be overwhelmed and destroyed by evil, so that his cross could be the means of destroying evil, and the symbol of its destruction.

Jesus conquered evil by his perfect human trust and obedience to his Father. He let his human heart be totally filled with his divine power and love.

So the Christian "answer" to suffering is, "Trust the Father as Jesus did on the cross."   .

But not all of us are able—at least not all the time—to accept the Christian answer. In the face of senseless suffering, tragedy and cruelty, something wants to whisper at the back of our minds, "If God is so good, how can you say that he 'permits' such evil? Why doesn't he stop the torture of the innocent, the hopeless pain in thousands of bodies, the insane malice that spreads through the world, the death of a young father or an innocent baby?"

Most people are not driven to despair by this question. If they do not have the perfect trust just described, neither do they have the defiance of Camus' "Stranger," raising his fist in the face of the "sublime indifference of the universe."

Somewhere in the middle of the spectrum, they just say, "It's God's will." If a business venture fails, it's God's will. If a woman dies in childbirth, it's God's will. If a plane crashes, it's God's will.

Is this faith or fatalism, or a mixture of both? I am sure that in most cases faith is the major ingredient. But sometimes the phrase seems to imply that life has all been pre-programmed on a cosmic computer, and that a million million events are predetermined.

We are (implicitly) compared to actors in a play, with no freedom but to say the words and perform the actions already laid out by the author.

I say "imply" and "implicitly" because we would not accuse God directly of heartless management of the world, or of a mechanical scheduling of precious human lives. But we do live in a world where people still say that if the bullet has your name on it, you will die, and if it doesn't, you can run through a crossfire and never get hit.

"It's God's will," then, can be a symbol of Jesus' total trust in God, or it can be (without being explicitly recognized) a way of blaming God for essential human limitation (the supply of oil runs out) or human error (a car accident) or the inheritance of others' sin (death) or the result of one's own sin (drinking oneself to death).

The trouble is, God never defends himself when any or all of these things are "explained" with a few quick words, "It's God's will."

In the past, during several retreats, I have made the mistake (from one point of view) of saying what I will attempt to say now, namely, that God does not *schedule* a list of sicknesses, accidents and deaths that are all going to happen as surely as tomorrow's sunrise.

After almost every one of the discussions that followed, someone was sure to come to me and say, "You have just taken away the only crutch I had to explain the death of my baby!" I will never forget one woman, crippled from birth, whose face was flushed with what must have been terror. She had always been taught that God had a "special reason" for her affliction, and I had contradicted that teaching.

Some people would observe at this point that no one should take the statements of any one priest so seriously. I agree. But I know that many people do take the statements of their priests very seriously— not as many Catholics as formerly, but enough.

Let us try to get a clearer focus on this problem before going on. Unless a priest simply gets up in church and reads from the Bible or the documents of Vatican II or other councils, I think it is impossible to exclude the influence of his own personality on what he says. (Even if he only reads the Bible, his pauses, emphases, etc., would affect the way the message comes through.) His choice of examples, his conclusions, his suggestions for practical application of the gospel come out of his temperament, history, values and experience.

So the very nature of preaching or writing involves personal emphasis, opinion and viewpoint, and a priest, or anyone, cannot continually be pointing out this fact. It should be evident that not everything he says is "official."

This discussion about "God's will," then, is my attempt to express what I believe is a theologically sound way of treating the subject. It is my opinion, if you will. I wouldn't be publishing it if I didn't think it had some merit. But I realize that many people will not agree. I heartily endorse their right!

## As the Bible Tells It

Let us begin with what seems to be the fundamental problem: two ways of looking at life. The first might be called the biblical outlook: The Jews simply saw God as doing everything.

God made it rain, and God drew the flowers from the soil; God decided victory or defeat in battle; God painted the sunset and brought the cedars of Lebanon crashing to the ground. God enfolded a baby at a mother's breast, and God "hardened" the heart of Pharaoh. God makes color TV, rainy days, arthritis, chocolate sundaes, dusty roads and taxes.

There are all kinds of examples in the Bible which seem to show God as a very active disciplinarian, sometimes zapping the Chosen People with wholesome punishments, at other times wiping out their enemies and sending manna in the desert.

The other way of explaining things, which does not necessarily contradict the first, thinks in terms of *secondary causes,* i.e., second to God. God is the source of all life, truth, love, power, everything. But he lets his creation follow its own nature. He doesn't build the robin's nest, but puts the instinct into the creature. He doesn't directly arrange the sunset every night, but lets the combination of nature's forces of light, wind, moisture, heat, etc., paint the nightly picture. It's his picture, and it's perfectly true to say, "Look at the beautiful sunset God has made tonight!" But it's also perfectly true to say that he does it through the nature he created, and the laws he inscribed on nature's heart.

One familiar example of the biblical outlook which we accept and understand, and yet interpret in a "secondary causes" way, is the account of creation. Our faith has no difficulty today in realizing that God may have taken millions of years—not seven days—to make the earth and man. He did not hang the moon in the sky one Thursday evening. And yet we can smile and agree with the explanation that God says to the sun every morning: "Get up and do it again!"

But sometimes, in pain and darkness, we take the extremely literal biblical view, *but only half way.* So we are able to "blame" God for cancer, unemployment, drought and someone's infidelity, while at the same time blithely asserting that God wants us to use our heads, and isn't it wonderful that we are able to achieve such amazing things as weather forecasting, moon flights, electron microscopes and computerized billing.

Poor God. We see only crosses as coming from the divine throne. God "sends" disappointments in love and business, "permits" parental cruelty and oppression of the poor. But God apparently has nothing to do with the warm sands of Miami Beach, the cheerful chugging of a Volkswagen, or the majesty of a Beethoven symphony.

We can't have it both ways. We must take either the biblical view that God is in everything, or another one (not contradictory) that sees God as offering us *the freedom and the power* to be his intelligent, loving and maturing children in a world that will always be cursed with human malice.

How do we go about absorbing the best of both views? It seems we have to consider several aspects of the question: (1) the foolishness of fatalism; (2) the kind of God we are dealing with; (3) the inevitability of suffering; (4) the risk of freedom; (5) the need to decide.

## The Foolishness of Fatalism

Taking a superficial view of "God's will" turns it into a cold, ruthless computer tape. According to this view, legions of angels (it would take millions) have somehow typed (or keypunched) a zillion zillion decisions of God. It's all set. The history of the world, and of our individual lives, is prearranged. According to this view, it is God's will that...

1) The State Street bus will hit Joe Banner at 5th and Main at 2:39 p.m., July 5, 1988.

2) Mary McCune must marry Pete Nitney at St. Margaret's, at 10 a.m., September 7, 1984.

3) A squirrel must eat through the wiring and cause a fire in your basement at 4:22 a.m., December 8, 1999.

4) Joe Schultz is going to flunk his algebra test.

5) A bullet is going to miss a thousand obstacles and

fall into the home of Marshall MacGruder, striking him on the left ear, at 1:10 a.m., July 7, 2010, because that is the day he is scheduled to die.

Had enough? Now consider that this is just an infinitesimal pinhead's worth of all the decisions God is supposed to have made from "all" eternity. There are four billion people in the world. They each live 24 hours a day. Each hour has 60 minutes. Supposing that there is *at least* one decision of God's will for every minute for every person, that means there are 5,760,000,000,000 items of "God's will" on that computer tape for just *one day.* For a week, a month, a year, for the history of the world—there is no number big enough.

(Now you know what thunder is. It's the noise of moving in new computers up there. The end of the world will come when there's no more room, even in heaven, to store the tapes.)

Isn't it marvelous that these trillions of pre-planned events come off so efficiently, when the odds are that one half contradicts the other?

So much for your name being on the bullet. Whatever God's will is, it's not ridiculous.

A priest friend tells me that this kind of criticism is too "man-centered." It supposes, he says, that because man can't handle the complexity, God can't either. But that's not the point. It is precisely because God is who he is that we don't want to distort his image into that of the Super-Arranger in the Sky.

### Who Is This God Who Has a "Will"?

As soon as we say "God's will," we seem to be

47

talking about two things. First, there is God, a benevolent Father looking out benignly over the blue-green earth. Then, God has a "will," over which even he seems to have no power, since he apparently, somewhere back there, decided everything once and for all.

Theologians have to keep reminding us that we can't get God into 30 or 40 catechism definitions. God transcends all human attributes. His life is infinitely more alive, free, happy, loving, wise, etc., than we can possibly imagine.

So it is important not to think of God "using" his free will the way we do. Our human wills are moved by what they *lack*. I *want* happiness, acceptance, love, forgiveness because I don't have it, or not enough of it. But God, being God, is life without limit, love without limit, infinite happiness, self-possession. If this were not so, God would be incomplete, needing something, unfulfilled.

The great Christian revelation is that God is (to use human concepts) Father, Son and Spirit totally immersed in mutual love. God is, in some mysterious way, total giving and total receiving of love. God *is* love.

Jesus is the visible sign that God wants to have intimate union with human beings. He does not give them gifts, he gives them *himself,* his intimate life.

We must have a fundamental concept of God, then, before we approach other problems. Before we ask what God "wants" in this particular situation, before we look at the age-old problem of suffering, before we talk about punishment and law and sin, we must have an absolutely clear picture that God is Personal Gift. God is Love offering endless friendship, life, happiness, vision, fulfillment. That is the nature of God.

Recent theologians have tried to help us soften our cold and formalistic idea of God by telling us that God loves us *passionately.* Human passion is physical-emotional-spiritual, of course, and is subject to change. But if we can keep the notion of intensity, warmth, fire, endlessness, then we can have a glimmering of God's "passionate" love for us.

If you listen to St. Paul, there is a simple answer to what "God's will" is: "It is God's will that you grow in holiness" (1 Thessalonians 4:3a). Holiness means letting ourselves be possessed by God's kind of living, loving, knowing and "feeling." It means, like the human Jesus, to be totally open to all God has to give, and then to act with God's power, led by God's light, to grow in his life by treating others the way he treated them—especially in the model of Jesus.

*That's God's will, whatever else it is.* Any further specification of God's will must never contradict this fundamental fact.

### Then Why Doesn't God Stop the Suffering and Cruelty?

The Cross is the only real answer to the problem of suffering. But we can also attempt a philosophical answer, a "secondary causes" answer if you will. It won't make much of an impression on a woman being beaten by her husband, or a man being slandered out of a job, or a wife visiting her husband in a mental hospital.

But it is a valid argument. It's the *freedom* argument, and it runs like this:

Supposing that God wants beings in his image, fully human, able to choose, to love, to trust and thus to grow to mature union with him, he must give them freedom to choose. If he were to install a freedom-removing gadget in human nature that would automatically prevent anyone hurting anyone else, he would no longer have human beings, but robots. Take some examples:

John Smith is going to murder his employer. God now has two choices. He can himself kill John Smith (painlessly) or "fix" his mind and emotions so that he doesn't think about his employer any more. He just keeps going to work unthinkingly.

Helen Jones is going to abandon her husband and children and start living with a "lover." Again, she either drops dead (hardly a solution) or God erases all her emotions and plans, and she stays (divinely brainwashed) with her husband.

A drunken man swings an ax handle at the head of another man, but God makes him miss, even at a two-foot range, or he shuts off the anger before it starts.

And so on. Bullets change course, or drop softly to the ground, while the gunman forgets why he pulled the trigger. Hatred gets mysteriously dissolved in the mind. The lie comes out truth.

The process will get more complicated when God not only must prevent millions of evil human actions, but must produce good actions in those who sin by omission. The man who never has a kind word for his wife will have to get a kindness-shot from God, which will produce a moderate amount of verbal comfort for the lonely spouse. The lad whose laziness adds to everyone else's work will get a sort of supernatural adrenalin that will make him rise and shine.

And we'll all live happily ever after. Well, not exactly happily. We'll all live mechanically ever after. A race of robots, with no problems. A universe of perfect machinery. Cities filled with mechanical men and women like those manufactured by General Electric for Disney World. No muss, no fuss. No pain and no sin.

No nothing.

The first comment one must make about this world of bionic bumpkins is that God certainly could do a better job, if that's the kind of world he wanted. Obviously that was not what he had in mind.

## The Risk of Freedom

God took an unbelievable risk. We would never go that far. He willed beings like himself—free, intelligent. He wanted mature, loving children; that is, children who would love him by their own choice— not to get the lollipop, not like trained dogs, not like slaves fearful of the whip—but as true lovers.

So God revealed himself gradually over the centuries. When the time was ripe, he revealed himself perfectly in Christ—and yet not perfectly (i.e., with nothing hidden or mysterious). There is a vision not yet seen, and there is a kind of darkness where only trust can operate.

There must be a space, a distance, for trust to walk through if God is not to smother us with his love. There must be some darkness for faith to wait in, lest the light of God blind us into adoration we have not had a chance to choose.

So what is God's will? That there be *human* beings—mature, aware, understanding, humble, unselfish, trusting, kind, patient, forgiving, courageous—like himself.

*By the same token* there can also be human beings who can freely choose to be selfish, cruel, greedy, lustful, etc. No one can be a saint unless it is possible to be a sinner. If there could be no cowards, there could be no heroes.

So God lets freedom be. It's worth the cost. Rather, free, loving human beings are worth the cost.

### Jesus Came to Restore Our Freedom

In discussing freedom as we have, there is the danger that it all sounds "neutral," like a new blackboard on which both good and bad can be written, or like a new instrument that may or may not work. In fact, the situation that already exists is that our freedom has been damaged. We are born into a world whose very structures can be evil, some of them totally infected with greed, selfishness, cruelty, injustice. There is great pressure on us to go along with this world.

But beyond that, each of us allows his freedom to be more or less straitjacketed by habits of feeling and thinking and deciding that are determined not by any virtue of prudence but by willfully ignoring facts and truth, and enjoying lazy rationalizations of our selfishness.

God did indeed take a risk when he made us free: the risk that we wouldn't accept freedom. His

52

greatest desire—his "will"—is indeed that we be *free*. Jesus' life, death and resurrection were for the purpose of *liberating* us from sin and Satan, from slavery and death. But this is possible only if we let him liberate us from our own selves. Salvation means being freed. God isn't so much worried about what we might do with our freedom as that we might do nothing at all with it.

So God lets freedom be—the use and the abuse—but he does not contemplate mankind's self-imposed slavery with a helpless gesture of despair. He does not presume that all those who are injured by the abuse of freedom will be satisfied with this rational "freedom argument" we have been trying to present. God lets the abuse of freedom do its worst. And it will do that worst until the end of time. "Truth forever on the scaffold, wrong forever on the throne," as James Russell Lowell said.

Death and sin and suffering have all been destroyed. But we will have to wait to see the "outside" of Christ's victory over them. *The "inside" is already here: it is his dynamic overflowing presence within us by his power and truth and love, and his call to us in every circumstance of life.*

To those who will accept it, God gives a life and a spirit, a power and a vision, that cannot be conquered by evil. It is a spirit referred to by Thomas Merton: "The silence of God embraces us, consoles us, answers our questions (once we have the sense to stop asking)." This is the power the Spirit of God pours into the hearts of men and women through the saving body and blood of Christ.

In Jesus, God puts himself on our side. When our lives are blighted by the abuse of freedom, he enters into the resulting pain. He is on the side of the suffering, the maimed, the deprived, the cheated. And he himself becomes the strength whereby freedom can flourish and be divine even in agony. He suffers as we do, he is destroyed by death as we are. He experiences the cruelty of hate and unfaithfulness, the senseless pain of whipping and crucifixion, the humiliation of ridicule and spittle on his face.

God's face.

It is simply unthinkable to put God on the "other" side of suffering, like the sadistic Nazi doctors who experimented to see how long human beings could live in icy water.

We are tried by fire, but not because God planned it that way. It is true that human beings can be ennobled by suffering, but not because God worked out a schedule of pain for testing us. Even in a sinless world, a space for trusting would have been necessary, and a little darkness, at least, for faith to penetrate.

It was in the trusting heart of Jesus that the victory was won. And as it was with Jesus, so it can be with us, if we have his spirit.

So, Jesus the *suffering* savior is God's answer to suffering. This is the Jesus who *had* to suffer, as the Scripture says. He *had* to suffer because only if he entered into the worst of our enslavement could he gather us together in the depths of our misery and offer to lift us up. He laid down his life alongside all the other sufferers of the world. He let men lift him up, like an insect on a stick, knowing that his Father would lift him up all the way to a new and liberated life.

Jesus could say to Philip, "Whoever has seen me

has seen the Father" (John 14:9b). The Father loves you so much that he gives you his Son. *God* suffers on a cross. If you want to know how the Father loves you, I am the sign." The cross was not a vindictive Father's pound of flesh. It was the divine scheme to conquer evil by letting it "conquer" everything but freedom in the heart of Jesus.

And when he had won the victory of a loving, trusting human being over death, he remained incarnate in human pain through his Body the Church. The Church is that group of people (hopefully someday all people) who say, "Do you want to know how Jesus loved, forgave, trusted, endured? Look at us. Do you need the healing, comforting hand of God to sustain you in your pain? We are sent by Jesus to be that."

So, just as Jesus said, "If you want to know the Father's love, look at me, the Church." The people of the Church are called to be the visible, healing, comforting, sustaining, sympathizing, understanding presence of Jesus. The Church, like Jesus, is God's answer to suffering. It does not explain suffering. It conquers suffering by enduring it with divine courage.

So the rational explanation of freedom merges into the religious explanation of the Incarnation and death of Jesus. And the "answer" Jesus gave must be given by the Church. In a word, suffering can only be borne if there is a sign of divine presence through other human beings. If the Church—that is, Church people—do not see this as their primary earthly way of honoring God, they will never reach a suffering world.

# Natural Catastrophes and God's Will

There is an area of human suffering that is not the result of the abuse of human freedom. People can freeze to death in a blizzard, babies can drown in a bathtub, fire can destroy a whole family, an earthquake can swallow up a city.

The freedom argument will not work here. But a similar one must be attempted.

God made a material world, and matter has its own natural laws. A stone sinks in water, flowers need sunshine, a fish cannot live on the land. Man's stomach will accept certain things as food, others it will not. Friction causes heat, fire consumes, bees sting.

Since the earth was formed in fire, its surface plates will shift in the cooling, and giant fissures may appear—earthquakes. Heat and cold give birth to the wind, sometimes driving wind that can lift houses and twist oak trees out of the ground. Fire consumes whatever is available to it. In short, if God makes a stone, or water, or sodium, he lets each one's nature take its course. To want him to be perpetually "tinkering" is to question the very wisdom of creating these things in the first place.

But you'd better have the Cross, rather than this argument, when an earthquake destroys your town.

I do not mean, by all this meandering discussion, to demean the faith of the young widow mentioned earlier. Some of the greatest inspirations I have had in my life have come from the tremendously powerful faith of good people who remain gentle and patient, trusting in God in the midst of tragedy, senseless suffering and loss. They are able to say, simply,

"It is God's will." It must be true that they do not mean that God has a list of scheduled sufferings and planned tragedies. I am sure they are not contriving groundless "explanations" to cover despair or bitterness or fear.

Rather, they have learned the lesson of the Cross, the only "explanation" of suffering. They are able to enter into the mystery of the heart of Christ, pierced and destroyed by evil, yet ultimately victorious. He did say, "My Father, if it is possible, let this cup pass me by" (Matthew 26:39). But his greatest words were, "Father, into your hands I commend my spirit" (Luke 23:46). He challenges us to say along with him: "Father, I put my life into your keeping. Father, I entrust myself to you. I take my body, my spirit, and put it into your hands."

At the heart of Christian faith is trust. Not a make-believe attempt to say that "God must have a good reason" when we are certain that he does not, but an absorbing of the wholehearted trust of Jesus in his Father.

Christians do not explain suffering. They look from their own cross to that of Christ and believe that suffering and death lost their sting because he let them conquer him. He took the worst of mankind's sad inheritance and maintained in his heart and mind a simple, perfect, human, loving, trusting union with his Father. That saves us, when we absorb the same attitude.

Our life, then, is constant growth in knowing the real God.

# 4. Prayer of Petition

## Then why pray?

**O**ne problem (among many) may still linger in many people's minds: Given the understanding of God's will and man's freedom outlined in the preceding chapters, what place is there for *asking* God to do something, stop something, or give something?

If God lets people and things follow their nature, and if God does not withdraw his gift of free will even when we decide to abuse it, then *isn't prayer of petition futile?* Why ask God to *do* something that would involve tampering with free will or nature (e.g., sending rain, sunshine, employment, happy marriage, safe trip, passing grades) or to *stop* something that would involve breaking into the natural course of events or human freedom (e.g., ending war, sickness, hate, floods, drought, cancer)?

God *does* allow human freedom to make its own choices, and he does not take back his gifts of freedom when his will is rejected.

Ordinarily he does not stop bullets or slanderous remarks. We need not say that God had a *special* reason why the bridge of San Luis Rey collapsed (it was old and rusty) or why John Kennedy was shot (an evil or demented man was out to get him) or why my mother died of a stroke. Natural causes take their toll. God does let things run.

We are treading on sacred and sensitive ground here, but it does not seem necessary—in fact, it leads to hopeless dilemmas—to say that God's tender and personal love for me will make him quench every unkind word aimed at me, or head off every germ. Our loving Father did not annihilate the monsters at Buchenwald, create rice for the babies of Bangladesh or loosen the locks on the "tiger cages" in Vietnam. God did not do these things, and certainly many holy people prayed that he would.

What these questions do is force us to understand prayer of petition in a broader context. True, it is *futile* to expect God to change his mind (i.e., act as if men did not have free will, begin intervening in the course of nature as if creation didn't operate by its own internal laws and exigencies). True, it is *unnecessary* to inform God of our needs, as if he might not know or care without our prayers. But prayer of petition should be much more than this. This chapter will try to say what that "more" is.

# Legitimacy of Prayer of Petition

Does prayer of petition, then, have a place in Christian life? Absolutely! To deny this would be to fly in the face of Jesus' clear command and promise: "Ask, and you will receive . . . . For the one who asks, receives . . . . If you, with all your sins, know how to give your children what is good, how much more will your heavenly Father give good things to anyone who asks him!" (Matthew 7:7, 8, 11).

There is a very important condition attached to Jesus' promise: Christian prayer is made in the name of Jesus—that is, with his attitude, his vision, his purpose and his grace. We will discuss this condition later. But the statement still stands, and we begin our discussion with the certainty that Jesus told us to offer prayers of petition.

Even though our heavenly Father "knows what we need before we ask him," and loves us better than we love ourselves, our psychological-spiritual health demands that we *express* the truth of our lives: We are 100 percent dependent on God. The fundamental reason for prayer of petition, then, is that we need to articulate our total dependence.

Even an atheist psychologist would tell us this. Whatever is truly a part of our deepest human convictions *must come out.* It seems that nothing is fully human until it is expressed externally, by word, act, concrete decision. There is no such thing as a man "presumably" loving his wife. If he never looks at her, or speaks to her, or kisses her, he does not love her. It's not only murder that will out: everything must come out, or it isn't "in."

So, if the most basic fact of our existence is that

we are constantly being held in existence by the loving, creative and sustaining act of God, and if this is the most basic fact of our consciousness, then it will come out.

The wisdom of centuries of Christian life has always expressed this in prayer of petition. Obviously we don't have to inform God of our needs, still less persuade him to take care of us. It is to preserve and deepen the *consciousness* of our need of him that we keep on "asking" for everything.

Objectively, it is easy to say that we need God's help 100 percent. Who would dare deny it? But psychologically, all the evidence, it seems, is to the opposite. It is *my* decision to get up and go to Mass. It is *my* magnanimous choice to forgive my unlovable brother-in-law. It was *my* fully-conscious will to sit up all night with a sick friend. How can anyone say that I "needed" God to do these things?

I might grudgingly admit that I needed God to get the whole thing started. But when it's a question of coming through with results, please don't tell me I need something called grace or outside power, like a crutch or a shove, to do what was obviously under my control.

The temptation to think this way is the crux of human life. Sin is the refusal to accept God *totally*. Faith is admitting what sounds illogical: My "free" action is a gift of God. Everything is God's gift—even the ability to pray for God's gifts.

So my very prayer of petition is a gift of God, as well as my fundamental need to keep on saying that I need him: for my next heartbeat, for the power to think and walk and love and work—for everything.

Therefore at the end (or better, the beginning) of

my prayer for this specific thing, I must have the deliberate (and immensely relieving) consciousness that I simply want to tune in on God's wavelength, be open to his gift. Or rather, to let him tune *me* in.

To say that no prayer is genuine unless it is inspired by the Holy Spirit is to say that all prayer is a response to something God does first. All prayer is grace. It's not *mine,* really.

God's enabling love precedes all I do, even though my prayer may seem to be as spontaneous as a tear, or as determinedly my creation as a visit to the dentist. All our actions are re-actions. Theologian Karl Rahner says, "Our prayer for grace is based on an unasked-for grace which gives us the power to pray and the act of praying itself. Of ourselves we would always turn away from God if God's grace did not anticipate us."

A remarkable line in one of the Eucharistic prefaces says, "Our desire to please you is itself your gift." Paradoxically, I need to keep saying, for *my* spiritual health, "Please keep giving me my desire to please you," even though God wants to give it more than I want to receive it.

This explains what otherwise might seem a curious way in which the Church prays. Many of the prayers of the Mass are asking for what we are already being offered. If there's any problem, it's on our part: "Remember all of us gathered here before you"; "Let your Spirit come upon these gifts to make them holy"; "Look with favor on your Church's offering"; "Give us strength to grow in love"; "Direct your love that is within us"; "Father, eternal Shepherd, watch over the flock redeemed by the blood of Christ"; "Let the Spirit you sent on your

Church continue to work in the world."

All of which may teach us that the best way to petition is *as* the Church and *with* the Church.

## A Basic Supposition About All Prayer

It will be helpful for all of us to step back from the prayer of petition and see it in the light of a fundamental truth of faith: We do *nothing* for our salvation by our own strength. Everything good we do is not our creation but God's gift. "Without me you can do nothing." We find it very hard to take that word *nothing* seriously.

Now if everything good towards our salvation is the gift of God, then certainly the most important element of our salvation—prayer—is the gift of God. Humanly, we are tempted to think that prayer is what *we* do. Then God "answers." Do we really believe that we do not even *begin* to pray, however reluctantly, unless we are already being inspired and strengthened by God himself?

Every single one of us should probably stop right here and spend some time trying to believe this with our heart. It would make all the difference in the world if we were really convinced that prayer is not our doing, still less our problem, but God's graciously given gift. I am being allowed to enter into communion with the Almighty. I am not a protestor trying to break into the manager's office; I am a guest whom the manager meets at my home and brings to his own home.

If I really believed this, what a difference it would make in *what* I ask God for, and *how* I address my petitions: not angrily, or with any fear that

I really can't "get to" him; still less with a paranoid feeling that he always "sends" me large troubles and small blessings.

So when I pray for a better job, it is my Father in heaven who is giving me the light and the strength to pray for a better job! It is an astounding thought.

*How* do I "let" God help me pray? Even that is his gift. But by a mysterious combination of his grace and my freedom, when I pray for Joe Smith to be elected to Congress, Jesus' own spirit and Spirit, power, love and life enter into mine.

What happens, or what should happen? I see my desires set against the background of all God's concerns, his patience, his gift of freedom, his wisdom.

I still pray that I get a better job, but with what an altered consciousness!

## A Still More "Unbelievable" Truth

If "prayer as gift" is hard for us to take, our minds are "blown" by another fact God has revealed to us: *The Holy Spirit prays our prayer!*

St. Paul writes to the Romans: ". . . we do not know how to pray as we ought; but the Spirit himself makes intercession for us with groanings that cannot be expressed in speech. He who searches hearts knows what the Spirit means, for the Spirit intercedes for the saints as God himself wills" (Romans 8:26-27).

Do we really consciously believe this? It is God telling us, in the inspired Scripture, that the Spirit is the one who prays, if prayer is truly prayer.

This means that a truly Christian prayer of petition (say, for a job, or for a safe delivery, or for guidance in making a decision) *is prayed* within us by the Holy Spirit of God himself!

How can God pray to God? Here we are in the mystery of the Trinity, and the first answer is, "We don't know." And yet, since we do know there are three Persons joined in an eternal interchange of love, it is not beyond imagining that Mrs. Jones' worry about her son in South Africa is the *shared concern* of Father, Son and Spirit.

If such is my belief (and it is that of millions, surely) then I feel myself, as it were, "in on" the consciousness and love of the Trinity. What a *possessing* thing it is to know that God worries with me, cares with me, suffers with me.

When I pray for my mother's recovery from cancer, then, the deepest knowledge of my heart is that the Spirit brings the redeeming and healing power of Jesus to the world. My love for my mother is deepened by being joined to the Spirit's infinite love and concern for her.

Dare we say that when Paul speaks of the Spirit "groaning" within us he is expressing God's own pain at the inevitability of evil in the world, once the gift of free will was given?

The Spirit is more concerned about my mother than I am. By the death and resurrection of Jesus, my mother's body will absolutely be freed from all pain and disfigurement and be radiant forever. Will some of this glory—at least earthly health—come soon? I don't know, but I am not self-righteously "resigned," still less in a mindless "stupor" of resignation. I can *rest* in the Spirit without needing an explanation or an "answer."

If the world thinks this is naive, "pie in the sky,"

the world is merely following its own limited vision, its own values.

But how do I know that God is really in-spiriting my prayer? How do I know that I am responding to grace and in grace? Maybe I'm merely being selfish, or childish.

We are faced again with the Godwardness of prayer. I am not trying to twist God's arm; I am really not trying to get something for my isolated self, even if I am asking for holiness. I am, as a creature, ultimately asking for the glory of God. So, to be sure my prayer is within the grace of God, my first concern should be that *God* is loved, honored, praised, glorified. Jesus taught us this in the Our Father. I must simply trust that God creates my good will.

I must constantly challenge myself that the opposite may be true, or partially true: I may merely be attempting to make God over into an idol of my own, a vending machine from which I can magically get whatever I please.

I can never really know for sure—a cleansing and chastening influence on my prayer.

So, prayer is not a call for help (as if I were stranded on a desert island), but *God's* attempt to persuade my free will to surrender to the healing power of his love. Prayer, even the most ardent prayer of petition, is an acknowledgement of the fact that we receive all from God—life, meaning, freedom, prayer.

Two definitions of prayer are thus understandable: "Prayer is the joyful acceptance of the fact of being created" (Rahner); "Prayer is a state of consciousness within which the mind and heart are open to perceive the fundamental union which exists between God and the soul" (*Desert Silence,* Place-Riordan).

Accepting our creaturehood means being keenly alert to what God wants to do with our gift. We seek the purpose for which God made us—but not necessarily the emotional satisfaction of personal "fulfillment." We simply desire that God be God, and that all things converge around this center.

Saints are people who see their own poverty and dignity (i.e., creaturehood), the total receiving-ness of being a creature, and let God make them pure receptacles.

Does this mean that St. Francis would not pray to be rid of his terrible headache, or that his friend Jacoba might be able to sell her house? No, but his prayers would not be *isolated* from his total Christian spirit. They would fit into the whole picture, like one passage of a symphony.

### Double-Talk?

But isn't all this pussy-footing? Anyone who is really holy, it seems to say, doesn't really ask for anything but God's will. St. Catherine does not *whole-heartedly* pray that Siena be saved from the plague.

If we mean by "whole-hearted" that she sees *nothing else* but the plague, that it must *absolutely* be stopped, that God *must* do this, that it would be unworthy of God if he refused, etc., then we would say that she did not pray "whole-heartedly."

But the word means what it says: *whole.* St. Catherine's *whole* heart looks at the *whole* picture.

She says: "If the plague is stopped, may your people love and praise you. If it comes, may your people love and praise you. For you alone are holy, you alone are Lord."

What perfect prayer of petition does, from our point of view, is express our naked clinging to life. We are saying that our self-preservation is not an *independent* value. Whether we live or die, God be loved. If the storm is averted, it is by God's love. If it comes, God's love is no different than before. In either case, our loving God is more important than any earthly happening.

When a mother prays that her son return safe from war, she is saying that her son's earthly and eternal health and happiness are the gift of God. She is saying that she knows God is more concerned for her son than she is. She is joining the love of God for her son. If her son is killed, she will cry, but the closeness of God's Spirit will be greater than her pain. Her prayer, and its answer, is joined to that of Jesus. She has been with him in agony, and now already shares some of the peace of the resurrection.

So the second presupposition of prayer of petition is that we look at the *whole* picture. We pray as those who know that there is an *end* coming. This prayer steps away from history into eternity, and prays for the world that began and ended. It takes God's viewpoint on that span of hours, and enters into God's perfectly wise guidance of that world *in view of the end*. The coming of Jesus will be God's definitive answer to *all* prayer. Then, through his life and death and resurrection, all petitions will be seen to converge on the one petition: "Father, may you be glorified, may your will be done."

## We Really Cannot Know

This brings us back to the phrase "God's will."

Father Karl Rahner reminds us that the prayer, "Not my will but thine be done" is not made in a *stupor of resignation,* meaning that the "resignation" is fine, but "stupor" is a befogging of the human mind and heart that God wants to be alert and open.

Our act of trust is not made by denying our intelligence. The word *resignation* can be used in a mildly paranoid way that implies that God is being slightly unreasonable, but (sigh) we will go along with him anyway. We put God in the category of all the people we must humor along: Cousin Obadiah insisting that horseradish will cure bunions; Uncle Pete insisting on a re-run of "Petticoat Junction" when everyone wants to watch the World Series.

In other words, we almost put God in the class of office managers who hand down directions that can only mean: "There's no reason for it, it's just our policy."

The "stupor" of resignation presumes there's some "unreasonable" reason why God does what he does. But faith and even human imagination tell us that we really *cannot* know what is best at any given moment. What appears real and important in our clock time may not be truly such in the timeless reality of God's view.

Father Romano Guardini has said, "He [God] does not work as man does with his tools, but in a thousand mysterious, subtle and hidden ways, *through the very essence of things.* We do not know whether the shape we want to give to events in a particular situation will really lead to the proper solution. Our lives do not obey the laws which govern business or professional work, where plans are drawn up and put into effect—more or less successfully as the case may be. Only a small part of what happens in our life results from what we see and understand; the other, and greater, part comes from unseen realms. It is to the unseen—the mystery of God—that we must direct our prayers."

When our petition ends with "Not my will but thine be done," we are not "giving in" to a cold-blooded and rigid "God's will." It is one thing to say I cannot plumb the depths of divine wisdom and love; it is quite another to say that divine decision is ground out in a heartless computer.

God is Mother Teresa wishing she could pick up all the abandoned babies in the world and nurse them back to health; he's Tom Dooley crying because there aren't enough hospitals in the jungle; he's a mother anguished because she can't substitute her own heart for the failing one in her baby.

But God "can't" do all that. So he took flesh in Jesus and did something about all the pain and death in the world by absorbing and destroying it in his mortal and risen body.

If we can let our faith possess our prayer of petition, we cannot really have any problems about free will, "the course of nature" or suffering. Even in pain, we rest in trust. The light of our faith tells us that our asking—as long as we try to make it humble and trustful—is not a grubby little human thing we have managed to create, but a gift of God. We believe that the very Spirit of God prays in us and with us and for us. We are in tune with the wisdom and love of God.

71

We still hope for what we want, but a yes is not crucial, for there is always something infinitely more precious to us than even the temporal life of a loved one, or the (temporal) relief of suffering, want, injustice. We take the eternal view which knows that all prayer for the destruction of evil and sin and the relief of all suffering *has been answered*. God's infinite power and justice will destroy all evil, and all prayer for relief and forgiveness and happiness—the prayer of Jesus—is already answered, and the answer is being brought to fullness as the Day of the Lord approaches.

### In Jesus' Name

If we absorb the full meaning of prayer as a gift, as a sharing in the Spirit's own action, the "condition" Jesus attached to getting what we ask is seen not as a restriction but as another roadsign to the peace of faith. It's not as though God said, "I'll be generous *but* . . ." Rather, he wants us to have the spirit and vision which can be ready for, and really want, the best and greatest good he can give.

"Whatever you ask in my name I will do" (John 14:13). This is not an invitation to a celestial fishpond. It is a plea from God to ask him for what he wants to give us most, the gift that only faith can see: God himself.

Notice the same intensity of desire in Jesus words:

. . . whatever you ask the Father,
he will give you in my name.
Until now you have not asked for anything in my name.

72

Ask and you shall receive,
that your joy may be full. (John 16:23-24)

If a million dollars would make us happy, God would come running with it. But he wants our joy to be *full*—of himself.

Other seeming reservations are similar invitations to fullness:

If you live in me,
and my words stay part of you
you may ask what you will—
it will be done for you. (John 15:7)

Either this is arrogant nonsense, and (as Saint Paul said of belief in a non-existent resurrection) "we are the greatest fools on earth," or we have here a glimpse of an ever-widening horizon, a horizon that merges into the infinite. The problem is not how to get our prayers answered; rather, the privilege is that we may live in Christ, and his words may actually stay part of us! Then we will know how to petition.

The same fact of divine life is also found in John:

Your fruit must endure,
so that all you ask the Father in my name
he will give you. (15:16b)

With the faith-view of petition we are not primarily concerned about getting something for ourselves, even something terribly important. Rather we are most concerned about the Kingdom, about God's wise, beautiful, eternal plan to be fulfilled in the lives we read about in the daily newspaper, and in those about us, and in ourselves.

We then understand the heart of the Lord, human and divine. The answer to my prayer is a greater likeness of my heart to the heart of Jesus. I know how concerned he is about all the things I want. I experience and in a way understand *how* he is concerned. I sympathize and empathize with his *caring*—so much deeper and more generous than mine—so that I need never worry about the "answer."

For prayer is *my* answer, not God's.

I really want Mrs. Jones cured. I really want the war stopped and my brother back at the family table. But I know God wants it more than I do. I enter into his healing, saving, caring heart.